Fasting
the Biblical Way

A Cookbook Based on Daniel 1:12
Erica Basora

That's Love Publishing

Scan for Free Campanion Guide

Introduction to Fasting the Biblical Way

Welcome to a unique culinary journey inspired by the scripture in Daniel 1:12, where Daniel and his companions choose a path of simplicity and purity in their diet amidst the luxury of the Babylonian court. This cookbook reinterprets their choice as an elimination diet, focusing on nourishing and wholesome foods. Unlike traditional fasting, which often involves abstinence, this approach emphasizes mindful consumption of plant-based, nourishing foods.

This is more than just a collection of recipes; it's a guide to integrating physical and spiritual well-being. Each recipe is crafted with the principles of Daniel's diet in mind, offering a harmonious blend of flavors and ingredients that are as satisfying to the body as they are enriching to the soul. This cookbook invites you to rediscover the connection between the food we eat and our inner life, blending culinary delight with spiritual depth.

Embark on this journey of culinary exploration and spiritual reflection. "Fasting the Biblical Way: A Cookbook Inspired by Daniel 1:12" is not just about cooking; it's an invitation to a lifestyle that honors both body and spirit. Let the story of Daniel guide you in experiencing the joys of a diet that is both simple and profound, nourishing both the body and the soul.

Welcome

Welcome to Fasting the Biblical Way: A Cookbook Based on Daniel 1:12. My name is Erica, and I am excited to bring you this cookbook. As a nurse, author, publisher, mom, and God's girl, I have been on my own spiritual journey for many years.

I believe that prayer and fasting can be powerful tools to help us grow closer to God, to gain insight into His plans for our lives, and to receive the blessings He has promised us. I also believe that when we approach these practices with an open heart and with faith, they can bring a greater understanding of who we are in Christ.

I hope this cookbook becomes a catalyst to help you on your journey of spiritual growth and maturity. That you may learn how Daniel fasted and apply this practice and discipline in your own life. May God bless you abundantly!

That's Love,

Erica Basora

CONTENTS

Zucchini Noodles with Pesto

SERVES: 6   **PREPARE TIME : 15 MINUTES**   **COOK : 0 MINUTES**

Ingredients

For the Pesto:
2 cups fresh basil leaves
2 cloves garlic, minced
¼ cup water

For the Zucchini Noodles:
4 medium zucchinis
Cherry tomatoes for garnish
(optional)
Fresh basil leaves for garnish
(optional)

Directions

Make the Pesto:
1. In a food processor, combine the fresh basil leaves and minced garlic.
2. Pulse until the mixture becomes finely chopped.
3. With the food processor running, slowly drizzle in the water until the pesto reaches your desired consistency.

Prepare the Zucchini Noodles:
1. Wash the zucchinis and trim off the ends.
2. Using a spiralizer or a vegetable peeler, create zucchini noodles by slicing them into thin strips. If you have a spiralizer, follow the manufacturer's instructions.
3. Place the zucchini noodles in a large bowl.

Combine the Pesto and Zucchini Noodles:
1. Add the prepared pesto to the zucchini noodles and toss until the noodles are well coated with the pesto sauce.

Serve:
1. Divide the pesto-coated zucchini noodles among four serving plates.
2. If desired, garnish with halved cherry tomatoes and fresh basil leaves for added flavor and color.

Stuffed Portobello Mushrooms

SERVES: 4   **PREPARE TIME : 15 MINUTES**   **COOK : 35 MINUTES**

Ingredients

4 large portobello mushrooms
2 tablespoons water
1 small onion, finely chopped
2 cloves garlic, minced
1 red bell pepper, diced
1 zucchini, diced
1 cup spinach, chopped
½ cup cherry tomatoes, halved
½ cup chopped fresh basil

Directions

Prepare the Portobello Mushrooms:
1. Preheat your oven to 375°F (190°C).
2. Clean the mushrooms by wiping them with a damp cloth. Remove the stems and gently scrape out the gills using a spoon. Place them on a baking sheet lined with parchment paper.

Prepare the Filling:
1. In a large skillet, heat the water over medium heat.
2. Add the onion and garlic and sauté for 2-3 minutes, until they become fragrant and translucent.
3. Stir in the red bell pepper and zucchini. Cook for another 5 minutes until they start to soften.
4. Add the spinach and cherry tomatoes. Cook for an additional 2-3 minutes until the spinach wilts and the tomatoes soften.
5. Mix in fresh basil. Cook for another 2 minutes to combine all the flavors.

Bake:
1. Stuff each mushroom cap with vegetable mixture, pressing it down gently.
2. Place the stuffed mushrooms in the preheated oven and bake for 20 minutes or until the mushrooms are tender and the filling is heated through.

Serve:
1. Remove the stuffed mushrooms from the oven and let them cool for a few minutes.
2. Serve hot as an appetizer or side dish for your Daniel Fast meal.
3. Enjoy your delicious Stuffed Portobello Mushrooms made with wholesome, Daniel Fast-friendly ingredients!

Cucumber and Tomato Salad Cups

SERVES: 4   **PREPARE TIME : 15 MINUTES**   **COOK : 0 MINUTES**

Directions

Prepare the Salad Cups:
1. Start by washing and peeling the cucumbers. If you prefer, you can leave some strips of skin for a decorative touch.
2. Slice both ends of the cucumbers and cut them into 2-inch thick cylinders. Then, carefully scoop out the seeds using a small spoon to create a hollow cup in each cucumber slice.
3. Place the cucumber cups on a paper towel to drain any excess moisture.

Prepare the Filling:
1. Dice the tomatoes into small pieces and place them in a mixing bowl.
2. Finely chop the red onion and add it to the bowl with the tomatoes.
3. Toss in the freshly chopped parsley and mint leaves.

Assemble the Salad Cups:
1. Carefully spoon the tomato salad mixture into the hollowed cucumber cups. Fill them generously.

Serve:
1. Arrange the cucumber and tomato salad cups on a serving platter.
2. Garnish with additional mint leaves and parsley for a pop of color and freshness.
3. Serve these refreshing cucumber and tomato salad cups immediately as an appetizer for your Daniel Fast, or as a light and healthy snack.

Ingredients

For the Salad Cups:
2 large cucumbers
2 medium-sized tomatoes
½ red onion
¼ cup fresh parsley, finely chopped
¼ cup fresh mint leaves, finely chopped

Scan for Free Campanion Guide

Baked Kale Chips

SERVES: 4   **PREPARE TIME : 10 MINUTES**   **COOK : 15 MINUTES**

Ingredients

1 bunch of fresh kale (about 8-10 large leaves)

Directions

Prepare the Kale:

1. Preheat your oven to 350°F (175°C).
2. Start by washing the kale leaves thoroughly and then pat them dry with a clean kitchen towel or paper towel. Make sure they are completely dry to achieve maximum crispiness.
3. Carefully remove the tough stems from each kale leaf. You can do this by folding the leaf in half lengthwise and running your fingers along the stem to separate it from the leafy part. Discard the stems and tear the kale into bite-sized pieces.

Bake:

1. Line two baking sheets with parchment paper or silicone baking mats. Spread the kale leaves out in a single layer on the baking sheets. Make sure not to overcrowd them.
2. Place the baking sheets in the preheated oven and bake for 10-15 minutes or until the kale chips are slightly golden. Be sure to keep an eye on them as they can go from crispy to burnt quickly.

Serve:

1. Remove the kale chips from the oven and let them cool for a few minutes on the baking sheets. Once cooled, transfer them to a serving bowl or plate.
2. Serve your baked kale chips as a healthy and delicious Daniel Fast appetizer or snack. They are best enjoyed right away but can be stored in an airtight container for a day or two.
3. These baked kale chips are not only a great appetizer but also a nutritious and guilt-free snack option during your Daniel Fast. Enjoy their savory flavor!

Divine Butternut Squash Soup

SERVES: 6   **PREPARE TIME : 15 MINUTES**   **COOK : 30 MINUTES**

Ingredients

2 tablespoons water

1 onion, chopped

2 cloves garlic, minced

1 carrot, peeled and chopped

1 medium-sized butternut squash, peeled, seeded, and diced

4 cups vegetable broth (no sodium)

Directions

1. In a large pot, heat the water over medium heat.
2. Add the onion, garlic, and carrot. Sauté for about 5 minutes, until the vegetables are softened and the onion becomes translucent.
3. Add the diced butternut squash to the pot. Stir well.
4. Pour in the vegetable broth, ensuring all the vegetables are submerged.
5. Bring the mixture to a boil, then reduce the heat to low. Cover the pot and let simmer for 20-25 minutes, or until the butternut squash is tender and easily pierced with a fork.
6. Use an immersion blender or transfer the soup in batches to a blender or food processor to puree until smooth. Be cautious when blending hot soup.
7. Return the pureed soup to the pot if necessary.
8. Ladle the Divine Butternut Squash Soup into bowls.

Garden Greens Smoothie

SERVES: 2 **PREPARE TIME : 10 MINUTES** **COOK : 0 MINUTES**

Directions

1. Place all the ingredients in a blender.
2. Blend until smooth. Add more water if needed.
3. Pour into a glass and serve immediately.

Ingredients

2 cups fresh spinach
1 cucumber, chopped
1 celery stalk, chopped
2 cups water
Ice cubes (optional)

Root Veggie Roast

SERVES: 4   **PREPARE TIME : 10 MINUTES**   **COOK : 40 MINUTES**

Ingredients

4 cups mixed root vegetables (e.g. carrots, parsnips, sweet potatoes, and beets), peeled and cut into bite-sized pieces

¼ cup chopped fresh parsley (for garnish, optional)

Directions

1. Preheat your oven to 400°F (200°C).
2. Spread the root vegetables in a single layer on a baking sheet.
3. Roast in the preheated oven for 35-40 minutes or until the vegetables are tender and slightly caramelized, stirring once or twice during cooking to ensure even roasting.
4. Remove the roasted root vegetables from the oven and transfer them to a serving platter.
5. Garnish with chopped fresh parsley, if desired, for a burst of color and freshness.
6. Serve the Root Veggie Roast as a delicious and satisfying Daniel Fast appetizer. It's packed with flavor and wholesome goodness.

Simple Steamed Greens with Garlic

SERVES: 4   **PREPARE TIME : 10 MINUTES**   **COOK : 5 MINUTES**

Ingredients

1 bunch of your favorite greens (e.g.,
kale, spinach, Swiss chard)
1 tablespoon water
2 cloves garlic, minced

Directions

Prepare the Greens:

1. Wash and rinse the greens thoroughly under cold water.
2. Remove any tough stems or ribs from the greens if necessary.
3. Tear or chop the greens into bite-sized pieces.
4. Fill a large pot with about an inch of water and place a steamer basket inside.
5. Bring the water to a boil over medium-high heat.
6. Once the water is boiling, add the prepared greens to the steamer basket.
7. Cover the pot and steam the greens for about 3-5 minutes or until they are tender but still vibrant in color. Be careful not to overcook.

Prepare the Garlic Seasoning:

1. While the greens are steaming, heat the water in a small skillet over medium heat.
2. Add the minced garlic and sauté for about 1-2 minutes, or until it becomes fragrant and lightly golden. Be careful not to burn the garlic.

Finish and Serve:

1. Transfer the steamed greens to a serving platter or individual plates.
2. Drizzle the garlic-infused water over the greens.
3. Serve the Simple Steamed Greens with Garlic immediately as a healthy and tasty vegan Daniel Fast appetizer.

Veggie-Stuffed Peppers

SERVES: 2   **PREPARE TIME : 15 MINUTES**   **COOK : 45 MINUTES**

Ingredients

4 large bell peppers (any color)
2 tablespoons water
1 small red onion, finely chopped
2 garlic cloves, minced
1 zucchini, diced
1 yellow squash, diced
2 tomatoes, diced
1 cup spinach or kale, chopped
1 cup broccoli florets, finely chopped
¼ cup fresh basil, finely chopped

Directions

Prep the Peppers:
1. Preheat your oven to 375°F (190°C).
2. Slice the tops off the bell peppers and carefully remove the seeds and membranes, setting the hollowed peppers aside. Optionally, chop the tops to add to the filling.

Prepare the Filling:
1. In a large skillet, heat the water over medium heat. Add the onions and garlic, sautéing until translucent.
2. Add the zucchini, yellow squash, tomatoes, spinach or kale, broccoli, and the chopped pepper tops (if using). Cook until all vegetables are tender but not mushy.
3. Sprinkle in the fresh basil and stir well to ensure everything is well combined.

Stuff and Bake:
1. Divide the vegetable mixture among the hollowed peppers, pressing gently to make sure they're fully packed.
2. Place the stuffed peppers in a baking dish, standing upright. Add a small amount of water to the bottom of the dish (about a ¼-inch) to help steam and soften the peppers as they bake. Cover the dish with aluminum foil or a lid.
3. Place the baking dish in the preheated oven and bake for about 30-35 minutes, or until the peppers are tender.

Serve:
1. Once done, remove from the oven and allow to cool for a few minutes before serving.

Mushroom and Veggie Medley

SERVES: 2   PREPARE TIME : 15 MINUTES   COOK : 15 MINUTES

Ingredients

2 tablespoons water

1 large onion, diced

2 cloves garlic, minced

2 cups button mushrooms,
cleaned and sliced

1 cup portobello mushrooms,
cleaned and chopped

1 zucchini, diced

1 red bell pepper, chopped

2 tomatoes, chopped

1 cup spinach or kale, roughly
chopped

Directions

1. In a large skillet, heat water over medium heat (instead of oil to adhere to the Daniel Fast guidelines). Add the diced onions and minced garlic. Sauté until the onions become translucent.
2. Add the button and portobello mushrooms to the skillet. Sauté until they release their juices and begin to brown slightly.
3. Add the zucchini, red bell pepper, and tomatoes to the skillet. Mix well and let the vegetables cook for about 5 minutes.
4. Finally, stir in the chopped spinach or kale. Cover the skillet and let simmer for another 3-5 minutes, allowing the greens to wilt and the flavors to meld together.
5. Once all the vegetables are cooked and the greens have wilted, remove from heat. Serve hot.

Bitter Greens Soup

SERVES: 2 **PREPARE TIME : 10 MINUTES** **COOK : 30 MINUTES**

Ingredients

1 large onion, diced

3 cloves garlic, minced

5 cups water, plus more for sautéing

2 cups kale, roughly chopped

2 cups mustard greens, roughly chopped

2 cups turnip greens, roughly chopped

Directions

1. In a large pot, add the onion, garlic, and a little water. Sauté until the onions are translucent.
2. Add the kale, mustard greens, and turnip greens to the pot.
3. Pour in the 5 cups of water and bring the mixture to a boil.
4. Once boiling, reduce the heat and let it simmer for 20-25 minutes.
5. Serve hot.

Dandelion and Radicchio Salad

SERVES: 2   **PREPARE TIME : 10 MINUTES**   **COOK : 0 MINUTES**

Directions

1. In a large salad bowl, combine dandelion greens, radicchio strips, cucumber slices, and chopped celery.
2. Toss the salad gently to mix the vegetables well.
3. Serve fresh.

Ingredients

2 cups dandelion greens, roughly chopped
1 head of radicchio, sliced into thin strips
1 cucumber, sliced
2 celery stalks, chopped

Bitter Melon Stir-Fry

SERVES: 2   **PREPARE TIME : 10 MINUTES**   **COOK : 10 MINUTES**

Directions

1. In a large skillet or wok, sauté onions and garlic with water until translucent.
2. Add the bitter melon slices to the skillet and sauté for about 5 minutes.
3. Introduce the broccoli florets and continue to sauté until the broccoli is slightly tender but still retains its bright green color.
4. Serve hot.

Ingredients

1 large onion, sliced
2 cloves garlic, minced
2 tablespoons water
2 bitter melons, sliced into thin circles
2 cups broccoli florets

Endi e and Watercress Salad

SERVES: 2   PREPARE TIME : 10 MINUTES   COOK : 0 MINUTES

Directions

1. In a large bowl, combine endive, watercress, cucumber slices, and celery.
2. Gently toss to mix the ingredients.
3. Serve immediately.

Ingredients

2 cups endive, chopped
1 cup watercress
1 cucumber, thinly sliced
2 celery stalks, chopped

Bitter Gourd and Brussels Sprouts Sauté

SERVES: 2 **PREPARE TIME : 5 MINUTES** **COOK : 10 MINUTES**

Directions

1. In a pan, sauté the onion with the water until translucent.
2. Add the bitter gourd slices and Brussels sprouts.
3. Sauté until the Brussels sprouts are golden brown.
4. Serve hot.

Ingredients

1 onion, thinly sliced
2 tablespoons water
1 bitter gourd (also known as bitter melon), deseeded and thinly sliced
2 cups Brussels sprouts, halved

Simple Arugula Soup

SERVES: 2   **PREPARE TIME : 5 MINUTES**   **COOK : 20 MINUTES**

Directions

1. In a pot, sauté the onions and garlic with a little water until soft.
2. Add the arugula and sauté until wilted.
3. Pour in the water and bring to a boil.
4. Simmer for 10-15 minutes.
5. Serve warm.

Ingredients

1 onion, diced
2 cloves garlic, minced
4 cups water, plus more for sautéing
3 cups arugula, roughly chopped

Chard and Broccoli Rabe Medley

SERVES: 2   **PREPARE TIME : 10 MINUTES**   **COOK : 10 MINUTES**

Directions

1. In a skillet, sauté the onion with water until translucent.
2. Add the chard and broccoli rabe to the skillet.
3. Sauté until both greens are wilted and tender.
4. Serve hot.

Ingredients

1 onion, sliced
2 tablespoons water
2 cups chard, stems removed
and leaves chopped
2 cups broccoli rabe (rapini),
chopped

Hearts of Palm Salad

SERVES: 2   **PREPARE TIME : 15 MINUTES**   **COOK : 0 MINUTES**

Ingredients

1 can (14 ounces) hearts of palm, drained and sliced into rounds

1 cup cherry tomatoes, halved

1 cucumber, diced

1 red bell pepper, diced

¼ cup red onion, finely chopped

Fresh cilantro, chopped (optional, for garnish)

Directions

1. In a large salad bowl, combine the heart of palm slices, cherry tomatoes, cucumber, red bell pepper, and red onion. Gently toss to mix well.
2. Garnish with freshly chopped cilantro if desired, and serve immediately.
3. This salad is light, refreshing, and perfect for a hot day or as a side dish to a main course. The hearts of palm add a unique texture and flavor, complementing the fresh, crisp veggies. Enjoy!

Scan for Free Companion Guide

Hearts of Palm "Rice" with Bitter Greens

SERVES: 2   **PREPARE TIME : 10 MINUTES**   **COOK : 15 MINUTES**

Ingredients

1 can (14 ounces) hearts of palm, drained
2 tablespoons water
1 large onion, diced
2 garlic cloves, minced
2 cups dandelion greens, roughly chopped
2 cups mustard greens, roughly chopped

Directions

1. After draining the hearts of palm, pulse them in a food processor until they reach a rice-like consistency. Set aside.
2. In a large skillet, add water, diced onion, and minced garlic. Sauté on medium heat until the onions become translucent.
3. Introduce the dandelion and mustard greens to the skillet. Sauté until the greens wilt down, which should take about 3-4 minutes.
4. Add the processed hearts of palm to the skillet, mixing thoroughly with the greens. Cook for an additional 5-7 minutes, ensuring the hearts of palm are heated through.
5. Once everything is well-combined and heated, transfer to serving dishes and enjoy immediately.

Simple Mushroom Burgers

SERVES: 2   **PREPARE TIME : 15 MINUTES**   **COOK : 10 MINUTES**

Ingredients

4 large portobello
mushroom caps
3 tablespoons water, divided
1 cup finely chopped
spinach
½ cup finely chopped
broccoli

Directions

1. Clean the mushroom caps with a damp cloth. Remove the stems and set the caps aside.
2. In a skillet, add 2 tablespoons water, spinach, and broccoli. Sauté until the veggies are softened.
3. Once the veggies are cool enough to handle, stuff the mixture into the underside of the mushroom caps.
4. In the same skillet, add a tablespoon of water and place the mushroom caps, stuffing side up. Cover and let them cook on low heat for about 5-7 minutes, or until the mushroom caps are tender and hold the shape of a burger.
5. Once cooked, you can place the mushroom burgers on lettuce leaves as a "bun" or enjoy as is.

Simple Veggie Stir-Fry

SERVES: 2   **PREPARE TIME : 20 MINUTES**   **COOK : 15 MINUTES**

Ingredients

2 tablespoons water

1 cup broccoli florets

1 carrot, thinly sliced on the bias

1 red bell pepper, sliced into thin strips

1 yellow bell pepper, sliced into thin strips

1 zucchini, sliced into half-moons

1 cup snap peas or snow peas

1 cup sliced mushrooms (like shiitake or button)

2 green onions, chopped (both white and green parts)

Directions

1. Be sure to wash and chop all your veggies in advance so they're ready to go. This is key to a successful stir-fry since the cooking process is fast.
2. In a large skillet or wok, add the water and bring it to a slight simmer. Add the broccoli and carrots first, as they take longer to cook. Stir-fry for about 2-3 minutes.
3. Add the sliced bell peppers and zucchini. Stir-fry for an additional 2-3 minutes, ensuring everything is mixed well.
4. Add the snap peas or snow peas along with the mushrooms. Continue to stir-fry for 3-4 minutes or until the mushrooms are tender and the peas are bright green and slightly softened.
5. Add the chopped green onions and give everything a good stir for another minute.
6. Once all the vegetables are cooked to your desired level of tenderness, transfer them to a serving dish. Enjoy the stir-fry while it's hot and appreciate the natural flavors and colors of the vegetables.

Spaghetti Squash Veggie Medley

SERVES: 2   **PREPARE TIME : 15 MINUTES**   **COOK : 55 MINUTES**

Directions

Prepare the Spaghetti Squash:
1. Preheat your oven to 400°F (200°C).
2. Cut the spaghetti squash in half lengthwise and scoop out the seeds.
3. Place the squash halves cut-side down on a baking sheet and bake in the oven for about 40 minutes or until the flesh is tender and you can easily scrape the strands with a fork.
4. Once cooked, remove from the oven and let it cool slightly. Using a fork, scrape the insides to release the spaghetti-like strands.

Prepare the Veggies:
1. In a large skillet, add the water. Once heated, add the broccoli florets and sauté for 2-3 minutes.
2. Add the sliced red bell pepper and diced zucchini to the skillet. Continue to sauté for another 3-4 minutes.
3. Stir in the cherry tomatoes and cook for an additional 2 minutes until the tomatoes are slightly soft.
4. Add the spinach and stir until it just begins to wilt.

Combine and Serve:
1. Add the spaghetti squash strands to the skillet and gently toss everything together, ensuring the vegetables are evenly distributed.
2. Transfer the mixture to a serving dish and enjoy the melding of natural flavors from the array of vegetables.

Ingredients

1 medium-sized spaghetti squash
1 tablespoon water
1 cup broccoli florets
1 red bell pepper, sliced
1 zucchini, diced
1 cup cherry tomatoes, halved
1 cup spinach

Daily Habits when Fasting

When devoting time to Prayer and Fasting each day you should
1. Spend time in communion with the Lord in prayer,
2. Spend time with the Lord by reading His word
3. Take time to journal and reflect on your spirtual journey

Pray for Loved Ones

Pray for your Petition

Spend time with the Lord in the Word

Take time to journal each day.

Scripture of the Day

Reflection

Scan for Free Campanion Guide

www.ingramcontent.com/pod-product-compliance
Lightning Source LLC
LaVergne TN
LVHW072116070426
835510LV00002B/84